LET US RISE UP . . . WITH A GREATER READINESS, LET US STAND WITH A GREATER DETERMINATION. AND LET US MOVE ON IN THESE

# POWERFUL DAYS

THESE DAYS OF CHALLENGE TO MAKE AMERICA WHAT IT OUGHT TO BE. WE HAVE AN OPPORTUNITY TO MAKE AMERICA A BETTER NATION.
—MARTIN LUTHER KING, JR.

Text by Michael S. Durham
Introduction by Andrew Young

# POWERFUL DAYS

## The Civil Rights Photography of Charles Moore

Stewart, Tabori & Chang   New York

Professional Photography Division
Eastman Kodak Company

To Dad, the Reverend Charles Walker Moore,
in loving memory,
for his gentleness and strength of faith
and his acceptance of all people.
— C. M.

Frontispiece: Martin Luther King, Jr., at a rally on the steps of
the state capitol in Montgomery, Alabama.

Text copyright © 1991 Michael S. Durham
Photographs copyright © 1991 Charles Moore

Published in 1991 by
Stewart, Tabori & Chang, Inc.
575 Broadway
New York, NY 10012
and The Professional Photography Division,
Eastman Kodak Company

Library of Congress Cataloguing-in-Publication data

Durham, Michael S. (Michael Schelling), 1935–
    Powerful Days : the civil rights photography of Charles
Moore / text by Michael S. Durham : by Charles Moore.
    Includes index.
    ISBN 1-55670-171-3—ISBN 1-55670-202-7 (pbk.)
    1. Afro-Americans—Civil rights—Southern States—Pictorial works.
2. Civil rights movements—Southern States—History—20th century—
Pictorial works.   3. Southern States—Race relations—Pictorial
works.   4. Moore, Charles, 1931– —Photograph collections.
I. Moore, Charles, 1931– .   II. Title.
E185.61.D94 1990
323.1′ 196073075—dc20                          90–10327
                                                CIP

Distributed in the U.S. by Workman Publishing,
708 Broadway, New York, New York 10003
Distributed in Canada by Canadian Manda Group,
P.O. Box 920 Station U, Toronto, Ontario M8Z 5P9
Distributed in all other territories by
Little, Brown and Company, International Division,
34 Beacon Street,
Boston, Massachusetts 02108

Printed in Japan
10 9 8 7 6 5 4 3 2 1

# Contents

# Preface

In the spring of 1988, I flew to New Orleans with my wife, Maryann, and from there drove a rental car through the southern coast of Mississippi and Alabama and along the beaches of Florida before turning north again into Alabama. I wanted to visit my son, daughter, and other relatives that live in my home state of Alabama; from there we would drive into Mississippi and down the Natchez Trace, on to Natchez and Vicksburg. We drove along a lot of the back roads and through small towns that reminded me very much of my childhood days. I marveled at the friendliness and hospitality of the people I came in contact with and could not help but think of the curses that so often greeted me in those turbulent sixties when I was on assignments with cameras for my newspaper in Montgomery and later for *Life* magazine.

It was a different spring in May of 1963, one that few people in Birmingham, Alabama, could enjoy; it was a time of high-pressure water hoses and snarling police dogs turned on people demonstrating for their civil rights and crying out for their human dignity. The South was about to change and this threatened change brought out fear, anger, and hatred in many white Southerners.

As a born and bred Southerner, I was often shocked at the behavior of some people in places like Selma, Birmingham, Oxford, and St. Augustine. Their faces, contorted in anger, threatened me and cursed at me. I was not the instigator of violence; I was there to record news events that were making history. For all journalists covering the civil rights story through the sixties, it was difficult, exhausting, and often very dangerous. For me, it was all the above plus troubling and emotional in a personal way because I am a Southerner, too.

Traveling through today's South I could not help but notice the obvious changes, such as integrated restaurants, motels, bus stations, and schools. Much slower in changing are attitudes. Some people's attitudes will never change, but I hope and believe that the civil rights movement has helped a younger generation understand the need for equality and justice for all people.

Pictures can and do make a difference. Strong images of historical events do have an impact on society. Our goal in bringing together these photographs in a single volume is to remind citizens of the South and this country that we must all move forward together without racism and bigotry so that future generations will live in a better, more peaceful world.

People are struggling for democratic reform around the world. The cry for freedom is heard from South Africa to the Soviet Republics. We must not give up our own struggles in this great country for increasing democracy and equality for all people. At times I feel we are a complacent society, and in complacency lies decay. Andy Young taught me a lesson one hot day in Birmingham, during the riots there. I had questioned the reasons men and women had for exposing themselves to the dangers of police dogs and high-pressure water hoses. Andy, in his cool and articulate way, explained the necessity of lives being put on the front lines to achieve justice and human rights: sacrifices were needed to make people aware of the need for change. Indeed, lives were lost in this struggle for justice.

Looking at these pictures and being reminded of the depth of commitment, I hope that we will be reminded of what can be accomplished when caring replaces complacency.

For the past year I have been lecturing at universities around the country, sponsored by the Eastman Kodak Company. I have shared my pictures and experiences with many bright young students who are both aware and concerned about our society. They are also very concerned about racism on the campus.

The University of Southern Mississippi specifically requested my presence to lecture and show my work. I was anxious about the reception I would get. The trip was like traveling back in time; I had not been in Hattiesburg since 1963. Memories of Oxford, Philadelphia, voter registration, and Medgar Evers' funeral accompanied me on my drive south from the airport in Jackson. After the lecture, the students' many questions and comments impressed me. White and black, they were honest about their need to continue improving racial attitudes in the community and their concern and willingness to confront difficult issues showed that progress had been made.

It has been enlightening and heartening to meet and speak with college students, some whose parents participated in civil rights campaigns, some whose parents opposed integration. I am convinced that these young men and women, black and white, are united in their desire to improve race relations in America. They are the future.

—CHARLES MOORE
Columbia, California
August 1990

# Acknowledgments

During my thirty-two year career as a photojournalist, many people have had a great influence on me, contributing to my growth as a photojournalist and human being. I would like to express my heartfelt gratitude to family, friends, and associates who have supported me and believed in me and my work. I thank them for their advice, inspiration, and friendship, and wish to acknowledge their influence on the contents of this book.

Howard Chapnick of Black Star is a man devoted to photojournalism; he has been my agent for the past twenty-eight years. Howard has given inspiration, support, and friendship to many young photographers searching for a path leading toward a photographic career. Special tributes must also go to Ben Chapnick, president of Black Star, for his support over the years, and to Yukiko Launois, the talented and dedicated photo editor, as well as to the many people at Black Star who have been like my second family.

Michael Durham was a reporter for *Life* and worked with me on a variety of assignments; he worked with me more than any other reporter on the civil rights stories and became a good personal friend. Michael urged me to collect my civil rights photographs in a single volume; he came to my home

and we spent many hours together beside a tape recorder discussing the events in this book, and from those conversations Michael has written an excellent text. He is a very good writer and editor, and I appreciate his friendship.

For help in identifying individuals in the photographs and in verifying aspects of the text, Michael and I both send special thanks to: Fred Bennette, Unita Blackwell, Hon. Hugh W. Clemen, Victoria J. Gray-Adams, Lawrence Guyot, Barnette Hayes, Mary King, Galway Kinnell, Pamela Clemson Macomber, Harriet Richardson Michels, Caryl Privett, Robert Zellner, and, at Black Star, Howard Chapnick and Annie Stewart.

I have watched the impressive career of Andrew Young since his days working with Dr. Martin Luther King. His energy and diplomacy left a lasting impression on me, and I credit him with helping me understand some of the methods of the civil rights workers. I am grateful to him for the kind words in his introduction and for the perspective his voice adds to this book.

I will always be grateful to the editors, reporters, and photographers of the weekly *Life* magazine. It was an honor to go on assignments for the best picture magazine in the world.

I am very pleased that this book is being published by Stewart, Tabori & Chang. It has been a rewarding experience working with Maureen Graney, senior editor, on this project; she has devoted much time and deep sensitivity to working with both Michael and me. Jim Wageman, the art director, has worked long hours on the design of the book. My deepest appreciation to both.

A special thanks to the Professional Photography Division of Eastman Kodak Company, who are co-publishers of this book. Kodak has also made it possible for me to lecture and share my work and experiences at universities around the country. I am indebted to Raymond H. DeMoulin, general manager of the Professional Photography Division and vice president of Eastman Kodak Company, for his strong support of photojournalism. Paul Curtis, market coordinator, photojournalism markets, and Ken Lassiter, director, photo trade relations, have been delights to work with; I value their friendship. I would also like to thank Ann Moscicki, director, worldwide sponsorship and special events, for the interest she had from the start in my photographs and for her support of the book.

Much credit for the success of my recent Kodak-sponsored lecture tour goes to Vern Iuppa of Iuppa/McCarten, who worked closely with Kodak and with me in many ways, from designing beautiful presentation portfolios for a special edition of my photographs to working out schedules to designing the poster for the lecture series.

I would like to thank Joe Holloway for introducing me to the world of photojournalism by hiring me as one of his staff photographers at the *Advertiser-Journal* in Montgomery; his enthusiasm always inspired me.

Thank you to Marty Forcher, not only for keeping my cameras in good working condition at Professional Camera Repair, but for his persistence in collecting and repairing broken down cameras donated by photographers and sending them to the civil rights workers in the south; his dedication to the cause will not be forgotten.

My brother, Jim, deserves special thanks for his inspiration and love; he has not only been my best friend, he has encouraged me throughout my career.

For Michael, Michelle, April, and Gary, my love and thoughts for all of you have traveled with me to the far ends of the earth. Thank you for your love and respect.

—C. M.

# Introduction

Some forty years ago, while I was a student at Howard University in Washington, D.C., I drove home to New Orleans for a brief vacation. Interstate highways were still on the drawing board in the early 1950s, so travel through the Deep South involved long stretches of two-lane blacktop and very few places for a young black man to stop.

In Georgia, the best thing to do was not to think about stopping—period. Crossing from South Carolina into Georgia on U.S. 29, I decided to turn around and get gas in South Carolina, wishing not to risk running close to empty in the Peach State. As I approached Atlanta well past midnight, a sewer rat crossed the street just in front of my car, which I was driving with extreme caution already. I slowed down to let the rat make it safely to the other side.

Rats had more rights than black people that night in Georgia.

If anyone had said to me, "Son, you'd better take your time and look around Atlanta, because you're going to be the mayor of this city one day," I would have called him crazy. Blacks could not even vote then. And yet, somehow, that same Georgia of which I was so afraid has become the home I love, the place where I have raised my family, and the birthplace of the greatest human rights movement in American history.

The photographs of Charles Moore presented in this brilliant chronicle offer more than simple, visual accounts of the civil rights years. First, for those of us who remember the pictured events from personal experience, this book is a means by which to sharpen memories, to relive and revisit some of the most meaningful, terrifying, and rewarding moments of our lives. The bravery and the beatings at the Edmund Pettus Bridge in Selma garnered the most national and international media attention since the fire hoses in Birmingham and in many ways stand as the strongest symbol of the struggle for the Voting Rights Act.

Selma reminds us of the quantum leap taken by the United States government following the passage of the act. The war on poverty, the attempt to open up educational systems, affirmative action, and realistic job opportunities—all were born from the Voting Rights Act.

These photographs also represent something more than visual history to a whole generation of black Americans, the generation of the 1970s and 1980s that has been the chief beneficiary of the struggle of the 1960s. Millions of young people today learn only from the history books that suffering and death were part of the movement. The educational and professional achievements of today's youth were never attained by Jimmie Lee Jackson, a young Vietnam veteran who was killed by a state trooper in Marion, Alabama, after participating in a voting rights march. Nor were the rewards of the movement enjoyed by Andrew Goodman, James Chaney, or Michael Schwerner, all of whom were murdered in Mississippi. A Unitarian minister from Boston sacrificed his life, killed while preparing to march from Selma to Montgomery.

These quiet heroes of social change died before their work was done, but they continue to provide us with inspiration and hope for our children's future. Dr. King said, "I may not get there with you, but our people will get to the Promised Land." When he too died, so much of the nation lost hope, lost inspiration, and wondered if the dreams for which he had fought would be buried with him.

Sitting in the White House Executive Office Building in the spring of 1978, ten years after his assassination, I became convinced that Martin's dream was indeed on the verge of becoming reality. I was the U.S. ambassador to the United Nations, presiding at a conference of more than a dozen White House staff members, all of them black.

I had asked to meet with the black staffers because I wanted them to realize that they were there as a result of the suffering and sacrifice of thousands of people of all races—people who had led our country to a confrontation with its Judeo-Christian conscience in the civil rights movement. Jimmy Carter was well aware that, as a southerner, his march to the presidency of the United States would have been impossible without the presence of the black vote and the achievements of Martin Luther King, Jr. But many of the young professionals on the White House staff had no such sense of history. They were the black youth who got their opportunity for higher education in 1968 when colleges and universities opened their doors to minority students, largely in the wake of Martin's death and the Kerner Report, the document that told of the two Americas, one black and one white.

The impressive fact to me was that I did not know any of them. They truly were a new elite, young people from a broad spectrum of the American landscape—small towns, urban ghettos, and western suburbs—who had obtained law degrees, masters, and doctorates from the country's finest schools.

Some of us have reached the Promised Land of equal opportunity and positions of power, but for many more the struggle for freedom flounders in a drug-induced slavery or wanders aimlessly in a wilderness of debt-ridden materialism. Indeed, the entire nation seems the captive of an economy distorted by needless militarism in other countries, a lack of direction and focus on serious social and educational dilemmas, and an absence of policy for burgeoning disasters in our environment.

The inflation and the unemployment of the 1970s produced large debt and a level of anxiety in our nation that caused us to turn our backs on the Great Society and become the Safe Society of need and greed.

Yet, amid all the false promises to the many and the sweet successes of the few, the struggle has continued. We have maintained in a quiet and persistent manner the rippling effects of the civil rights movement's tidal wave of change. It is slow and peaceful, but like "Ole Man River" it just keeps rolling along. The struggle has moved, by and large, from the front pages of newspapers and magazines and from the streets and courtrooms. Today, nearly thirty years after Charles Moore took these photographs, black politicians and decision makers fight alongside their colleagues in city council chambers, on the floors of statehouses, and in the halls of Congress. Though leadership from the White House has been virtually nonexistent, the movement has become so strong and secure politically, educationally, and economically that it pushed President Ronald Reagan to proclaim a national holiday in honor of Martin Luther King, Jr., and his nonviolent activities of social change. Even the Voting Rights Act of 1965 has been extended for another twenty-five years.

The problems, however, remain. The triple evils of racism, poverty, and war threatened the movement that began in Montgomery and Albany, and today they threaten it still. Legal segregation has almost completely disappeared, but the population is only beginning to appreciate the strength and beauty of ethnic and cultural pluralism.

With the continuing agony of poverty spreading to growing numbers of whites, the embers of smoldering racism occasionally flare up, but these are classic reversions to a desperate hooliganism among the victims of poverty. Certainly racial factors are involved, but violent crime, whether across racial lines or within racial communities, is much more the result of society's failure to house, educate, and employ our citizens.

In 1967, Dr. King spoke to us in our last staff workshop before embarking on the Poor People's Campaign:

> In the days ahead, we must not consider it unpatriotic to raise questions about our national character. We must begin to ask why there are 40 million poor people in a nation overflowing with such unbelievable affluence? . . . Why have we substituted the arrogant undertaking of policing the whole world, for the high task of setting one's own house in order? All of these questions remind us that there is a need for a radical restructuring of the architecture of American society. For its very survival's sake, America must re-examine old presuppositions and release itself from many things that for centuries have been held sacred. For the evils of racism, poverty, and militarism to die, a new set of values must be born. Our economy must become more person-centered than profit- and property-centered. Our government must depend more on its moral power than its military power.

But, to the end, Martin Luther King, Jr., remained

the apostle of nonviolent social change: "I must oppose still any attempt to gain our freedom by methods of malice, hate and violence . . . that have characterized oppressions. Like an unchecked cancer, hate corrodes the personality and eats away at its vital unity. It has no boundary lines."

The people shown throughout this book questioned many things about themselves and about their environment. Strength and knowledge came to them primarily through nonviolent participation in events that held unknown rewards and consequences. Sit-ins, marches, boycotts, citizen training, negotiations—whatever they chose as their movement endeavor, they experienced radical changes in their outlook on life.

Most of these people were volunteers, and that has been the case in the other major movements in which I have been involved: the women's movement, the peace movement, the human rights movement. America has always been led by volunteers, and they have not always been the older and most experienced individuals. So many times it has been the young men and women, employed in other fields, who have taken social change as the cause and meaning in their lives.

During my campaign for governor of Georgia in 1990, I was fortunate to enjoy reunions with many of these volunteer heroes of the civil rights movement as I traveled throughout the state. Indeed, I sometimes caught myself in a time warp, remembering faces and circumstances from the 1960s as I campaigned in Albany, Savannah, Liberty County, and Dawson, Georgia. How strange it was to make a stump speech about bringing a new day to Georgia on the steps of a courthouse where blacks had been turned away in their quest for the right to vote!

Letting that rat cross the street safely as I drove through Atlanta that night during my college days may have taught me more than I realized at the time about individual freedom and human rights. Many of us were treated like rats even during the most daunting days of the movement, as Mr. Moore's photographs of the fire hose attacks in Birmingham's Kelly Ingram Park so graphically illustrate. But faith and courage bolstered our desire, and the energy and inspiration we drew from Martin Luther King and others empowered us to see the battle to its conclusion. There are many more battles in which to engage as we approach a new century. All of us must hope and pray that the lessons learned and the lives lost during the first years of the movement will be remembered and honored to infinity.

—ANDREW YOUNG

# The Civil Rights Photography of Charles Moore

**1**

The turning point in the career of Charles Moore came amid pandemonium and violence on the night of Sunday, September 30, 1962. The place was the University of Mississippi; the story, the court-ordered admission of James H. Meredith, a twenty-eight-year-old air force veteran and a Negro, to the all-white school. Charles spent the night trapped inside the administration building with several hundred U.S. marshals, while outside a large and angry mob of whites attacked the building with rocks, guns, and incendiary bombs. The marshals had been ordered to Ole Miss, as the university is sentimentally known, to protect James Meredith and ensure his peaceful enrollment the next day. But all hopes of registering Meredith without bloodshed had long since vanished, and that night the marshals were fighting—with teargas and nightsticks since they were under orders not to use firearms—for their own survival.

As the only photographer inside the building, Charles emerged the next morning with an exclusive set of photographs that captured the drama of the siege; when they appeared in *Life* magazine the following week, they established Charles's reputation as a news photographer of unusual determination, talent, and daring. Charles spent the next three years in the front lines of the civil rights movement, often at great personal risk, covering stories as they unfolded for *Life* and other news magazines.

Charles had lived and worked in the South all his life, and he had known that Mississippians would not allow the university to be integrated without a fight. Blacks had tried without success to enter Ole Miss before, but Meredith arrived backed by a federal court order and accompanied by federal officials. Charles, a freelancer at the time in Alabama, drove over to Oxford, Mississippi, arriving just as the press was beginning to descend on the college town. Here he met the contingent of photographers and reporters from *Life*, then the country's largest weekly magazine.

At the time *Life* was trying without luck to persuade Ross Barnett, the segregationist governor who had twice earlier refused to register Meredith, to pose for photographers. *Life* was extremely unpopular with segregationists for the critical way its pictures and stories depicted racists and their violent resistance to the civil rights movement. Barnett, who owed his office to his support of segregation, refused to cooperate with the magazine.

When Charles learned that *Life* was unable to get access to Barnett, he told Richard Billings, who was directing the magazine's coverage, that he had contacts at the Mississippi statehouse from his days

Facing page: Inside the Lyceum, University of Mississippi, 1962.

with an Alabama newspaper. With Billings's go-ahead, he set up an appointment to photograph Barnett in Jackson, the state capital. When Charles returned to Oxford with film, Billings asked him to work exclusively for *Life* on the Ole Miss story.

By Saturday, September 29, tension was mounting throughout the state. The focus of events shifted from Oxford to Jackson, where Ole Miss played its football games. Although he was secretly negotiating with both President John F. Kennedy and Attorney General Robert Kennedy in Washington for a face-saving arrangement for Meredith's enrollment, Governor Barnett delivered an inflammatory speech to the stadium crowd: "I love Mississippi!" he shouted, as the crowd roared its approval. "I love her people! I love our customs!" Photographing on the streets of Jackson, where he had gone with the other *Life* journalists, Charles remembers:

**Beer-drinking college kids, lots of rebel flags, and little taunts at the press. The people were cheering more for Ross Barnett than for the football team. "Roll with Ross!" That was the big theme. . . .**

**I began photographing these three students who were each waving rebel flags. They started waving them at me, which was fine because it made dramatic photographs. But then they started jabbing—especially this one big guy—first at the camera, then at my face. Finally, I said, "Hey, wait a minute!" and raised up with my right hand real hard. I knocked one flag on the ground. I could tell from the way that they were looking that I had committed an unpardonable sin and that it was going to get bad.**

After this incident the *Life* reporters and photographers decided to regroup at their hotel room in Jackson. "From what had happened on the street, we could tell now it was going to get rough on the Oxford campus," Charles remembers thinking, when suddenly the hotel room door banged open and in rushed a phalanx of screaming college students, including the big guy with the flag, who

**came right at me and grabbed me by the collar and began twisting my tie and choking me. I've never been able to re-create the obscenities, but it was like, "You goddamn *Life* magazine bastards, we found out who you were. You nigger lovers had better go home."**

**I was thinking, I've got to be cool. This guy is husky, not much taller than me, but really strong. I'm getting flushed from anger but also from pain, so I reached up and grabbed him by his thumb and told him to turn me loose.**

**I never took my eyes off his eyes. I have never seen such hate on anyone's face before; it was as if I were vermin. I knew what he was thinking. To him I was worse than "a nigger," I was a white nigger . . . and worse than that I was a white *Life* magazine nigger. So I could tell he didn't care what he did to me.**

During the melee, a photographer from the Associated Press who had also been in the room began taking pictures, but the students grabbed his cameras and exposed his film. Charles's assailant was trying to force him to his knees, but as Moore, a former Golden Gloves boxer and an ex-marine, said, "There was no way he was going to do that." The incident ended when a state legislator, who had heard in the lobby what was happening, burst into the room and ordered the attackers out.

More aware than ever of the difficulties that covering Meredith's registration would present, the contingent from *Life* returned to Oxford, where the college town was filling up with U.S. marshals, state troopers, and white vigilantes, many of them armed, from around the state. On Sunday the police closed the campus in an attempt to keep away journalists and other outsiders. Posing as friends of a student journalist who had agreed to help them, Charles drove onto campus with Bob Fellows, a freelance reporter also working for *Life*.

The federal officials had made their headquarters in the university's administration building, known as the Lyceum. As the afternoon wore on, it became obvious that the building would come under attack. Moore and Fellows bluffed their way into the building by telling the marshal barring the door that Charles was desperately ill and had to use the toilet. Once inside, Charles recalls, "We stayed, and the marshal forgot about us."

The Mississippi state police had given up its efforts to keep troublemakers off the campus or even to keep order. As it began to grow dark, the crowd of angry whites outside the Lyceum began tossing rocks at the marshals and slashing the tires of the army trucks parked outside, the first acts of aggression in what would soon become a siege. Many in the unruly mob believed Meredith was inside the building (he was, in fact, under heavy guard in a dormitory on campus). Inside the Lyceum, Nicholas Katzenbach and John Doar of the Justice Department were on the phones keeping the Kennedys informed on the situation. When a marshal was knocked unconscious by a lead pipe thrown from the mob, the marshals retaliated with teargas. As Charles remembers it:

**As soon as it got dark, the scene became a nightmare. There was teargas floating on the air. We could hear shots being fired. Molotov cocktails were being thrown. Cars in the crowd were set afire. First the headlights would come on as the electrical system shorted out. Then the car would jiggle as the tires melted, then you could hear the tires pop. Then the gas tanks would explode, and people would have to jump aside. I could see things happening that I couldn't photograph. Also I couldn't spend much time out there; there was so much happening inside.**

When the firing started, Charles was standing on the steps of the Lyceum with William Crider, a reporter from the Associated Press. Charles ducked behind a Jeep; Crider turned and ran and was hit in the back by shotgun pellets. (Later that night Charles photographed the reporter, his bare back bandaged, interviewing marshals inside the Lyceum.) The rioters even brought up a bulldozer and threatened to advance on the building with it before the marshals managed to capture it. Inside the building all was chaos; Charles photographed a wounded marshal being treated and a prisoner vomiting from the gas into a wastebasket. As he described the scene:

**Inside there was teargas everywhere. The marshals would fire it into the crowd, and it would drift back into the building. Even when it settled you would stir it up by walking around. Most of the shots I took that night were made while I was wearing a gas mask. I had to guess at the focus.**

**They brought in one wounded marshal, who had been shot in the leg. They laid him down on the floor, ripped open his pants leg, and began working on him. Suddenly everything went black. I looked around and this big red-headed marshal had taken his hard hat off and stuck it right over my lens. Some of the marshals didn't particularly like the fact that we were in there, but I think finally they respected us for it.**

In all, 160 marshals were injured, 28 by gunshot. During the night the federal forces received word inside the Lyceum that a French journalist and a local repairman had been killed in the riot. Deputy Attorney General Katzenbach was eagerly awaiting the arrival of federal troops, which he saw as the only hope of restoring peace. Charles remembers hearing Katzenbach on the telephone, "pleading with Bobby Kennedy: 'They've got guns out there, Bobby, they've got guns. Our men are being shot.' He didn't want to use guns, but he wanted the marshals to have the right to defend themselves."

With dawn and the arrival of federal troops, the campus grew quiet. Charles and Bob Fellows left the Lyceum to cover the arrival of Meredith, escorted by chief U.S. marshal James McShane, for registration. Afterwards James Meredith was accompanied by U.S. marshals to his first class.

Although the press soon left Oxford, the military continued to arrive; over twenty thousand troops were at one time stationed in the vicinity of the university. Some five hundred were still there when Meredith was graduated in a peaceful ceremony the following August.

Once Meredith was enrolled and Ole Miss officially integrated, Charles flew on a private plane that *Life* had chartered to Memphis, where his film was shipped on to New York. For a major story, he had shot an unusually small amount of film—five or six rolls—but that and two cameras were all that he had been able to take with him when he sneaked onto the campus the previous day. In retrospect, he considers his shortage of equipment "good in a way":

**I wasn't encumbered by a big bag or a lot of different lenses. I couldn't shoot carelessly. (I could have easily shot off five rolls in the first hour.) I not only had to be more selective; with the gas mask over my face, I had to be more careful with focusing. Sometimes I just had to guess . . . and in available light, for I had no strobe with me.**

*Life* ran the Ole Miss story as its news lead the following week. Charles's eerie photographs, shot in the dim light of the teargas-filled Lyceum, dominated the article. The message conveyed by the images of the besieged marshals was loud and clear—and a foreboding of events to come: white Mississippi was willing to shed blood rather than give in to federal pressure to integrate.

**2**

Charles Lee Moore was born on March 9, 1931, in Hackleburg, a small town in northwestern Alabama, and grew up in nearby Valdosta, a community on the fringes of Tuscumbia, Alabama. His father, Charles Walker Moore, was the minister of a small Baptist church. Childhood pastimes included exploring caves by the Tennessee River, hunting with homemade bows and arrows, and competing and fighting with the boys from a similar white community nearby, Sugar Hill. Charles describes himself as "a real tough little kid who grew up in a community of tough kids."

know what it's like to wash in a dishpan. I know what it's like to go to the ice plant to get a block of ice to keep the food cool in the icebox, and I know what it's like to drink water out of a dipper. In fact, that's the best way in the world—to dip into a bucket of cold well water and drink it with a dipper. . . .

It wasn't an easy life, but it was a great life, because it was a family life.

Children of the rural South: Moore often photographed scenes, such as the one at right, that reminded him of the poor white community in which he grew up.

After Charles became a professional photographer, he often traveled the back roads of the rural South on assignments. He recently described these trips as "a little like traveling back in time":

Some of the houses I visited looked as good as any house I lived in when I was a little kid. We were poor— not dirt poor—but poor. We didn't have running water or a bathtub or a shower. We heated water in a tub on the wood stove. And when our well dried up, we had to walk to a neighbor's pump and carry the water back in buckets. I know what it's like to use an outdoor toilet. I

Charles's father was a gentle, soft-spoken Baptist minister—"not a hellfire and brimstone type"—and a man of tolerance and compassion. Charles remembers that his father never used racial epithets or allowed his sons to use them. "He called blacks 'colored folk,'" which was considered courteous usage in those days. Local churches were segregated, but Preacher Moore was often invited to deliver sermons at small Negro churches scattered about the countryside, and he frequently took Charles with him. Charles believes that his own racial attitudes were partially formed at these church services.

I remember going with my father and my brother to these little churches where everybody was black. Afterwards the black preacher would invite us to have dinner—that was what you call lunch up north—after the service. I remember one occasion; it was what they called "dinner on the ground," a potluck thing with the food on tables outside with singing. This is where I first heard gospel music, and I was absolutely

ored town" when he was about six years old. But to his young mind, whites and blacks "looked different and lived separately"; it was no more complicated than that.

Although blacks and whites came into daily contact in many ways, Tuscumbia was a typical southern town, and evidence of segregation was everywhere:

When he was still a newspaper photographer, Moore photographed these southern scenes: a mule and a rolling store, right, that served backcountry communities and two farmers, facing page, engaged in conversation.

amazed by the power in their voices. I knew church music, I knew "Rock of Ages" and "Amazing Grace" and all those other wonderful hymns. I still love them today, but more than anything else I love gospel.

Charles admits that, as a young boy, "I didn't dwell on the problems of blacks." He still has memories of playing when he was small with the black boy "who lived across the creek somewhere," and remembers the kindness of a black man who took him home when he lost his way and wandered into "col-

There was no mixing between blacks and whites. There were drinking fountains and toilets everywhere that had "white" and "colored" over them. In my naiveté and lack of knowledge of the world, I accepted this as the way things were. I didn't know any other way of life.

Years later, when he first went to New York City, another freelance photographer, who had invited him home for dinner, attacked him for having been complacent about segregation. In his own defense,

Charles tried to argue that, when he was growing up, "I didn't know that segregation was wrong." But his host was unconvinced: "Bullshit, you knew," he told Charles. The experience left Charles somewhat wary of northern liberals.

When Charles was about eight, his mother began a battle with cancer that would last until she died at

age thirty-two, five years later. The family had no insurance, so his father left the ministry to take a job as a car salesman to earn more money for the medical bills.

Even after his father left the ministry, Charles's life revolved around the church, with services on Sunday and sometimes a prayer meeting in the evening during the week. "Maybe I wasn't always aware of what was being said," he recalls, "but I was there." When he was age ten or eleven, he joined the church, but that decision became an increasing

source of confusion as he grew older: "If you did the least thing wrong—if you cursed, if you had a fight, if you did anything even slightly bad—you were constantly aware that, my God, this goes against everything I promised not to do."

When he was sixteen, he joined the Golden Gloves boxing team in a neighboring town. Charles quickly learned such rudiments as "never, ever let your eyes wander away from an opponent's eyes," and soon he was fighting competitively as an amateur welterweight. In two years he lost only three of thirty-three fights, one to a sailor—"an old man; he must have been twenty"—in Pascagoula, Mississippi. From boxing Charles gained confidence that "I could take care of myself," which would later stand him in good stead in the many dangerous situations in which he found himself as a professional photographer. It also helped him avoid some confrontations as a youth. "After I was on the boxing team, trouble just didn't happen around me; nobody wanted to mess with me."

Although he led much the same rough-and-tumble existence as every other kid in the community, Charles was aware from an early age that "there was more to life than just playing football and doing what the other kids were doing." He studied art with a local artist, took up magic as a hobby, spent hours at night gazing at stars, and dreamed of travel.

Charles traded an old autoharp ("we were always trading things") for his first camera, "a little Kodak Brownie." He processed his film by using "these little plastic dishes for trays and seesawing it right in the developer," and he made a crude contact printer from a cigar box and a twenty-five-watt bulb.

**Right from the beginning—even with the Brownie—I wanted to do something more than just point my camera and take straight shots of my family and friends. I would lie on the ground and shoot up. I would get up on the roof of the house and get my brother to stand with his arms crossed and look up at the camera so I could shoot straight down at him. And I'd have him get down in football positions: I'd get in close and shoot him from weird angles. He was my best subject.**

Charles soon acquired a better camera—"a $15 job called a Meteor"—and began working after school for two ex-GIs who had opened a camera shop in Tuscumbia. There he learned enough to pass the qualifying exam to train as a combat photographer when he entered the Marine Corps at age seventeen. He wasn't aware of it—"if anything, I wanted to be an artist"—but he was on a career path.

When Charles returned to Tuscumbia after the Marine Corps, being poor bothered him for the first time in his life: "I had become accustomed to hot water, refrigeration, air conditioning, and certainly indoor bathrooms, especially showers." He soon left for California, where he "studied portraiture and commercial photography and photographed every pretty girl I could find, because I wanted to be a fashion photographer" at the Brooks Institute of Photography in Santa Barbara. When his grandmother died a year later, he withdrew from Brooks to be with his father and brother. For a while he was adrift, selling insurance locally and representing a photography studio. Then, when his brother entered college on a football scholarship in 1957, Charles returned to photography, as a staff photographer for the Montgomery *Advertiser*.

**3**

By 1957 Montgomery, the capital of Alabama and a city that still proudly called itself the Cradle of the Confederacy, had already been a key battleground in the struggle for civil rights. On December 1, 1955, a forty-two-year-old seamstress named Rosa Parks had been arrested there after refusing to give up her seat on a crowded, segregated Montgomery bus to a white man. The protest that followed grew into the Montgomery bus boycott, which forced the integration of Montgomery buses a year later and brought its leader, Martin Luther King, Jr., to prominence in the civil rights movement. Charles, however, was mostly unaware of these events when he began working as a staff photographer for the Montgomery *Advertiser*. "I had no idea who Rosa Parks was," he recalls.

When he started at the newspaper, Charles says,

**I don't believe I was a very good photographer, but I quickly became one, because I had found a new love—photojournalism. It didn't take me very long to realize this was a whole different world, and that I loved it. I was becoming aware of what was going on, not just in Montgomery but in the country and in the world. Suddenly I found myself involved with blacks in a different way. Suddenly I was having to go out and photograph things that were happening between blacks and whites. I began to hear of this young dynamic minister, Martin Luther King, Jr., [King was appointed pastor of Montgomery's Dexter Avenue Baptist Church in 1954] and, having been the son of a Baptist minister myself, I was curious about this man.**

On one occasion Charles was assigned to cover a meeting of the Southern Christian Leadership Conference, the civil rights organization that Martin Luther King founded in 1957, in a country church north of Montgomery. The meeting had started by the time Charles arrived, and as he was parking his car, a white man approached and pointed a gun at him through the window.

**He asked, "Who are you, buddy, and what do you want?" I identified myself and said I was there on an assignment to take pictures of the meeting.**

**"You don't really want to do that. That's dangerous in there. Somebody could hurt you."**

**I said, "But that's my job."**

**"Well, I don't think that is a good idea. Who knows, somebody out here might want to hurt you."**

**"That's a chance I'll have to take. I have a job to do."**

**So he moved aside: "Okay, boy, don't say I didn't warn you." I just walked into the church and covered the meeting, which turned out to be no big deal.**

The incident gave Charles a foretaste of the hostility that he and the rest of the press would soon encounter as civil rights developed into a major story. Being arrested was another hazard of the civil rights story; a cameraman behind bars was in no position to record violence against demonstrators or other activists. Charles's first arrest came while he was covering a demonstration outside the Dexter Avenue Baptist Church in the late 1950s. He was quickly bailed out by the newspaper, and once he found a lawyer willing to defend his not-guilty plea (the newspaper's lawyer had advised him to plead guilty), the charges were dropped. Charles believed he learned a valuable lesson from the experience: "If you're in jail, you can't take pictures. After that, I tried hard not to give anyone an excuse to arrest me."

Charles's best-known picture from his newspaper days—taken on September 3, 1958—shows Dr. King sprawled across the booking desk of the Montgomery police station, his arm twisted behind his back by a policeman. King had been arrested while attempting to enter a crowded Montgomery courtroom with his friend, Ralph Abernathy, then pastor of Montgomery's First Baptist Church and an important organizer. (Abernathy had been subpoenaed to appear in a case involving an attack on him by a black man who believed Abernathy was having an affair with his wife.) As Charles remembers it:

**The courtroom was full, and King was on the little landing on top of the steps trying to get in. The police tried to run him off, but he said, no, he had his rights. Finally two policemen arrested him and hauled him off down the steps. As they started pushing him down the street, I ran along with them taking pictures. And when we got to police headquarters, I just ran behind the sergeant at the desk so I could get a shot of King bent over the counter as they booked him.**

After he was booked, King was taken to a back corridor, where he was frisked, roughed up, and thrown into a cell. The arresting officers apparently did not know who King was, but it did not take them long to learn. Soon afterward he was taken from his cell and released on his own bond.

Charles's photograph, distributed by the Associated Press, appeared in newspapers across the country and was responsible for bringing the national press to town for King's trial two days later. After he was found guilty of loitering and refusing to obey an officer, King, on principle, chose fourteen days in jail rather than pay a $10 fine and court costs. He also managed to deliver an eloquent statement expressing "my deep concern for the injustices and indignities that my people continue to experience" before the packed courtroom. The incident concluded on a bizarre note when Montgomery's police commissioner personally paid King's fine to "save the taxpayers the expense of feeding King for fourteen days."

In 1960, as sit-ins against segregated eating places spread rapidly across the South, thirty-five black students from Alabama State entered the basement cafeteria in the state capitol and left quietly when they were refused service. As modest as this protest was, it set the city on edge, and two days later, on a Saturday, groups of white vigilantes armed with small baseball bats were prowling downtown Montgomery looking for protesters.

Charles Moore and Ray Jenkins, city editor of the *Advertiser*-owned evening paper, the *Alabama Journal*, for which Charles also worked, were in the newsroom when they heard that trouble was developing between white vigilantes and black shoppers only a few blocks from the paper. The pair rushed to the scene just in time for Charles to grab a single shot of a white man swinging a bat at a black woman. The image, which ran in the next day's *Advertiser* and in newspapers across the country, has become one of the most famous photographs from the civil rights movement; that the angle of the photograph is askew only heightens the drama and sense of sudden and irrational brutality.

The *Advertiser* in this period was a typical southern newspaper: Democratic in its politics, enthusiastic in its sports coverage, and respectful of the southern way of life. One section of each issue of the newspaper was reserved for "Negro News." (Charles, promoted to chief photographer after a year on the paper, once had to threaten to fire a photographer who refused to take a picture for the section.) But despite the segregation within its pages, Charles believes that the *Advertiser*—in this period, at least—was impartial in its coverage of the civil rights movement.

**The newspaper tried very hard to portray everything fairly. It could have ignored the civil rights story; a very conservative paper would have said, "We're giving this troublemaker King too much publicity. Let's ignore him. Maybe it will die down." Well, the Montgomery paper didn't do that.**

When the newspaper published his photograph of the man attacking the black woman with a baseball bat—and named the attacker—Charles received a number of telephone threats on his life, and the police commissioner at the time, L. B. Sullivan, publicly chastised the newspaper for publishing the picture. The paper's editor, Grover Hall, eccentric, fair-minded, and outspoken, managed to put the situation into perspective. "Sullivan's problem is not a photographer with a camera," he wrote. "Sullivan's problem is a white man with a baseball bat."

**4**

By this time *Life* magazine had published a number of Charles's photographs, including his first images of the civil rights struggle. Seeing his own pictures in a national publication started Charles thinking about covering more than local events and about working on his own as a freelancer. In 1962 he took the first tentative steps toward this goal when he went to New Orleans on his own to shoot a photo essay on the nightlife of the French Quarter.

**For ten days I hung out with strippers, musicians, and bartenders, and when I left I knew I didn't want to go back to photographing accidents, and politicians, and society functions for the newspaper. I realized there was a larger world out there and I was determined to be part of it. So I started saving my money, and when I had $1500—in June 1962—I left for New York.**

New York proved an inauspicious start to his freelance career. Charles disliked nearly everything about the city—the heat, the noise, the crowds, and his apartment, "a fifth-floor walk-up in the East Village with one room and one window that was up against the brick wall of another building." With racial tensions building in the South, he was also aware of a certain amount of hostility toward southerners. One morning he found his Austin-Healey sports car, which was parked on the street, covered with eggs. Of course, he couldn't be sure, but he felt he knew the reason: his car had Alabama license plates.

Nor did the city seem to offer the opportunity he was seeking; making the rounds of magazines and photo agencies produced only a few small assignments, and his savings were dwindling fast. (At *Life* a junior editor politely looked through his portfolio—while he was having his shoes shined, Charles remembers.) Charles met many other young photographers and artists, but it seemed to him that many of them had been struggling for years without getting anywhere.

Only Howard Chapnick, president of the photo agency Black Star and representative of some of the country's finest photojournalists, offered any encouragement. Chapnick recognized Charles's potential; he also realized that the civil rights story was getting bigger and knew he would need photographers who knew their way around the South. So he offered Charles a small retainer if he would return to Montgomery. That was all Charles needed to hear:

**I moved out of my apartment in the middle of the night, and by daybreak I had reached the Chesapeake Bay Bridge. Once I was in Virginia, a southern state, I pulled over to a grassy spot on the side of the road and—I know this sounds corny—I got out and I grabbed grass and dirt, and said to myself, "Damn, this is good." Then I got in my car and drove back to Montgomery, back home again.**

Charles arrived back in Montgomery in August 1962 and immediately began to experience the bugaboos familiar to most freelancers: forced inactivity, financial insecurity, and self-doubt:

**I had been chief photographer in a town where I knew everybody, and suddenly I felt I was no longer part of the community. It was a lonely feeling. I missed the newspaper, and I had very little to do. At the time I thought I had probably made a mistake. I thought about opening a studio on my own, because I knew I would get business. But that's not why I quit the newspaper. I quit because photojournalism had become a love. So the rest of the summer passed slowly and painfully.**

But Charles proved his mettle with his unrelenting coverage of the resistance to James Meredith's registration at the University of Mississippi in late September 1962, and by November he was working as a freelance photographer in Miami, mostly for the *Life* southern regional bureau located there. Working out of Miami, Charles covered a whole range of subjects assigned to *Life*'s bureau as well as civil rights, an ongoing story.

In April 1963 the civil rights struggle seemed ready to explode. In Birmingham, Alabama, Martin Luther King, Jr., who had been organizing antisegregation protests by schoolchildren, was arrested on April 12 and from solitary confinement wrote his famous "Letter from Birmingham Jail," outlining his philosophy of nonviolence and civil disobedience. King was released from jail on April 20. Three days later William Moore, an eccentric postman from Baltimore on a solitary march against segregation through the South, was shot and killed on a lonely stretch of highway near Attalla, Alabama. The murder attracted national attention, and on May 1 ten volunteers from CORE and SNCC left Chattanooga to follow Moore's route, through Alabama, after cutting through the northwest corner of Georgia, to Jackson. *Life* sent Charles and a reporter from Miami to cover the march.

Today the march in the memory of William Moore through the heart of the segregated South is only a footnote in the history of the civil rights movement, but at the time it drew many journalists, some of whom had been covering the demonstrations in Birmingham. Violence against the marchers, who were eventually arrested by state troopers in Alabama, was considered a possibility, so, Charles recalls, "we kept parking the car, joining them, walking a little bit, and getting back into the car and driving—keeping close to them that way." The news on the car radio, however, was "all about Birmingham. Knowing the situation there [Birmingham was considered the most segregated city in America], and knowing about Bull Connor [the city's pugnacious police commissioner], I felt that we should be in Birmingham. So we just took off; I don't think we even stopped to call the office."

## 5

By the time King was released from the Birmingham jail on April 20, 1963, the SCLC was running out of adults willing to be arrested and jailed in the demonstrations. At the suggestion of James Bevel, an SCLC leader and an important figure in the events in Birmingham, the organization began to recruit high school students and even much younger children for its workshops in nonviolence and demonstrations. Even among Birmingham's blacks, the use of young children in demonstrations was controversial, but it did succeed in drawing the attention of the nation to Birmingham, which was exactly what the SCLC wanted. On May 2, the day before Charles arrived, over nine hundred young people cheerfully allowed themselves to be arrested.

On Friday, May 3, Charles and a *Life* reporter drove up to Kelly Ingram Park, the focal point of the demonstrations, just as firemen were bringing out their hoses in an effort to control demonstrators streaming out of the Sixteenth Street Baptist Church. Within minutes the firemen had turned the jets of water on the young demonstrators, producing scenes that outraged the nation.

**I recall driving into downtown Birmingham, seeing some commotion in the park, and jumping out of the car with my cameras. Things were already happening. I remember shooting the lead picture that appeared in *Life* right after we got there—of firemen leaning in and hosing down the blacks sitting on the sidewalk. There was no time to think about what was happening. I knew this was a bad situation and that I had to get in there and start taking pictures.**

The use of the high-pressure hoses on the demonstrators was the opening volley in a confrontation that would go on for the next five days. The demonstrators, many of them mere children, went about getting themselves arrested with good-humored restraint, but not all the blacks in Kelly Ingram Park that day had been schooled in Martin Luther King's philosophy of nonviolence. Soon young adults who had been observing the demonstrations were heaving missiles at the firemen. While he was photographing, Charles was struck on the ankle by a large piece of concrete.

**When I got hit, I was really angry, but I didn't know who to be angry at. I think I was mostly angry at the firemen, even though they hadn't hurt me. But I thought: if it weren't for what they were doing, the blacks wouldn't be throwing pieces of concrete, and I wouldn't have been hurt.**

That afternoon, demonstrators continued to emerge from the Sixteenth Street Baptist Church in well-disciplined platoons faster than the harried police could arrest them, while rioters kept up their barrage of rocks at the firemen. In an effort to contain the riot, Police Commissioner Eugene (Bull) Connor ordered police dogs into the fray. As the K-9 units lunged into the crowds, Charles took photographs.

The police dogs had an impact on Charles's journalistic detachment:

**My emotional involvement in the story grew as I saw what was happening. The police dogs were what really did it for me. I knew that those high-pressure hoses hurt people—I saw them ripping off their clothes, knocking them down, and rolling them around—but somehow I didn't see them getting hurt that badly. But the sight of snarling dogs, and the possibility of dogs ripping flesh, was revolting to me.**

On Friday evening Charles sneaked into a mass meeting that King was holding in the Sixteenth Street Baptist Church; the police had barred the press from the gathering, but a black man opened a window in back of the church to let him in. Charles describes the unforgettable scene:

**It was very hot and very emotional, with lots of singing and shouting out and amens. There was this one woman with a little child on her lap, and they were singing hymns and freedom songs and clapping and shouting, and the little kid was singing and clapping, and as I photographed the child, I began to choke up and my eyes filled with tears. It was very dark in there and**

**there was a lot of movement and I don't think I got very good photographs, but it was an experience I will never forget.**

By Saturday the demonstrators began converging on preselected points all over the city, where they would begin to demonstrate. This strategy kept the police—and the press—rushing frantically about. Even though he was limping badly from the shattered tendons in his ankle, Charles was determined to cover the story.

**There was so much going on at Birmingham, things were happening so fast—crowds would start running off in this or that direction—that the only way I could keep up with it was to run backwards and keep shooting. I wanted to be everywhere. And I didn't want to stand back and shoot it with a long lens. I didn't have much equipment at that time, no lens longer than a 105mm, but even a 105 would have kept me out of the action. No, I wanted to shoot it with a 35mm or a 28mm lens, to be where I could feel it, so I could sense it all around me and so I could get the depth that you get with a wide-angle lens. I wanted to see foreground, middle ground, and background. I wanted to get a feeling of what it was like to be involved.**

During the next four days, the violence of the riots dominated the Birmingham story, but peaceful protests continued. On Sunday the SCLC declared a moratorium on demonstrations, but the congregation of the New Pilgrim Church staged a spontaneous march to the jail. When they were stopped on the way by police and firemen, the line of worshipers kneeled and refused to move until Bull Connor, in a gesture that some of the marchers considered "a miracle," backed off on his threat to blast the marchers with fire hoses and granted them permission to enter a nearby Negro park to pray.

With the downtown area overrun by demonstrators and other blacks and the jails filled to beyond capacity, the SCLC, led by the always calm King aide Andrew Young, and a committee representing the white power structure moved haltingly toward an agreement on desegregation that would eventually end the demonstrations. Meanwhile the marches and the violence continued. As he was leaving the Sixteenth Street Baptist Church, Fred Shuttlesworth, a local minister who had planned the Birmingham campaign with King, was pinned against the wall of the church by a blast of water from a water gun. The minister was taken away in an ambulance, which prompted Bull Connor to declare: "I wish they had carried him away in a hearse."

Charles stayed involved in the Birmingham story until Tuesday afternoon, when he and the reporter took up a concealed position between two buildings, where Charles got close-up shots of a black woman being knocked down and skidded along the pavement by the fire hoses. When the police discovered they were there, the two journalists were arrested on charges of refusing to obey an officer.

**We had gone through the police dogs, we had gone through the fire hoses. We had gone through the emotions of the situation. But being arrested in Birmingham was one of the most dramatic moments in my career—also the most frightening. I have faced death and threats and all sorts of things—but this was scary. It was scary to be a victim.**

At the Birmingham jail, Charles was booked and locked up in a cell with a dozen or so young white men, all of them apparently angry at the overcrowding and judicial delays caused by the mass arrests of black demonstrators. One of them, Charles noticed with alarm, was trimming his nails with a pocketknife. He was well aware that civil rights activists in southern jails had been badly beaten on occasion by inmates, and he knew his fate could be the same if his cellmates learned the reason he had been arrested. As Charles later recalled:

**Two or three of the guys asked us, "What are you doing in here? You've got nothing to do with them demonstrators out there, do you?" They were angry, because the jail was packed full. And they knew there was all kinds of violence going on outside. I let them believe whatever they wanted, because I certainly didn't want them to know that we were from _Life_ magazine.**

Four hours later Charles and a writer jailed with him were bailed out by another _Life_ correspondent and released with an order to show up in court the next day. Back at the motel, on the phone with New York, the pair was advised by the _Life_ lawyer to get out of the state immediately, because a six-month jail term was likely if they went to court. When a local reporter questioned him as he checked out of the motel, Charles told him that he was going to spend the night in Montgomery with his family and would be back in time for court the next day.

**I didn't think he believed me, and I was worried; I knew it was possible that he would tip off the police, and as it turns out somebody did. As we were ap-**

**proaching the airport, a police car passed us going at full speed. When we arrived at the airport, there the police car was, empty, right in front of the entrance. I knew for sure that they were after us then. We left our rental car right in the parking lot with the keys in it. We knew we couldn't go into the terminal, so we walked down the side of the building until we came to an unused gate that opened on the central corridor—right across from the plane to New York. We checked in at the gate, and we boarded just as they were about to pull the stairs away from the plane. We flew away as fugitives from justice.**

In New York the *Life* editors had already laid out most of an eleven-page lead story on the Birmingham riots, which ran under Charles's byline. In the meantime, the lawyers told Charles not to return to Alabama until the charges were dropped (which they were after the *Life* team stood trial before a new judge about a year later). The year's wait was difficult for Charles; his children were in Montgomery, and Birmingham continued to be a center of turmoil and violence. On September 15 of that year, a bomb explosion killed four black girls while they were attending Sunday school at the Sixteenth Street Baptist Church. The tragedy caused Charles to reflect once again on his own upbringing and the existence of racism in a segregated South.

**The church bombing made me thankful that I had a father who taught me not to hate and that I never grew up with the kind of hate and bitterness that could turn me into a murderer of young children. Of course, I was on the verge of hate at this time—hatred of the racists who could bomb a church and kill little children. But I really never did come to hate them; I just couldn't understand them or how their minds had become so warped.**

## 6

The campaign against segregation and discrimination continued to build across the South during Charles's year-long exile from Alabama. The results were predictable—more violence—and President Kennedy's assassination on November 22 confirmed that political killing was becoming commonplace in America.

Almost six months earlier—on June 12, 1963—Medgar W. Evers, an NAACP leader from Mississippi, was assassinated by a sniper in Jackson. Evers was not well known outside the civil rights movement, but the fact that he was killed on the same night that President Kennedy broadcast a plea for "equal rights and equal opportunities" for all Americans shocked the country. Martin Luther King, Jr., was among the many leaders and dignitaries at the funeral, and the procession, recalled the comedian and activist Dick Gregory, "stretched so far back it looked like ants in a parade. . . . It looked like we had enough folks to march on God that day."

In late August of that year, more than a quarter of a million people, black and white, gathered in Washington to promote "jobs and freedom"—and the pending civil rights bill—in the most massive demonstration of political and ideological solidarity in American history. The March on Washington was organized by the venerable A. Philip Randolph of the Brotherhood of Sleeping Car Porters and his brilliant, controversial chief aide, Bayard Rustin, and brought together such black leaders as King, Roy Wilkins of the NAACP, John Lewis of SNCC, James Farmer of CORE, and Whitney Young of the Urban League. The march on Washington, which attracted celebrities and leaders from every walk of life, came to a climax with King's now-famous "I have a dream" speech.

Charles and a squad of other *Life* photographers were assigned to cover the event. In this case, Charles's fast-growing reputation as a photographer of action and violence worked to his disadvantage; his assignment that day was to stay on the fringes of the crowd to photograph any attacks on the marchers or other disruptions. There were none, despite apprehensions expressed by some of those who opposed the march, and the day was entirely peaceful.

But the march on Washington was an exception; most of the civil rights stories that Charles covered were risky and dangerous. This was particularly true for photographers; a person with cameras draped around his neck was an easy target. By this time Charles had developed a reputation for always being there when all hell broke loose. One network television correspondent so admired the way Charles maneuvered in fast-breaking situations that he would tell his crew to watch Moore and to move when he moved. But the possibility that he too might be a victim was never far from Charles's mind:

**I have been lucky that I have never been seriously beaten. I always knew that it was possible, but I never dwelled on it. I worried more about keeping my cool; I knew that I wasn't the type who could lie down and let somebody beat me—just because they were racist or because they didn't like who I was working for or because I was a "nigger lover," as we were sometimes called, or whatever—without taking up for myself. And I knew that fighting back would only make the situation worse.**

By and large the danger to journalists came from southern whites. The piece of concrete that smashed Charles's ankle in Birmingham was thrown by a black, but the intended target was more likely a fireman, not a journalist. White journalists, particularly from northern publications, were usually welcome in black communities and black churches, where so much of the civil rights organizing took place. Even the least sophisticated black person seemed to understand that most journalists sympathized with their cause.

In all the years he worked in the South, Charles was only attacked once. In the aftermath of sit-ins against desegregation in Jacksonville, Florida, in late March 1964, a black woman had been shot by police, and a bomb scare at a black high school had brought excitable teenagers out onto the street and into a confrontation with the police. Suddenly the police withdrew, and the students charged, overturning the press car Charles had been riding in and setting it on fire. As Charles remembers:

**I took off up the street. The kids were throwing rocks and bottles, and there was a lot of yelling and laughing**

31

and jeering. At one point I got behind a telephone pole and was leaning out to shoot when a rock or a brick smashed my 105mm lens. And then I started running again, and I could feel things hitting me on the back. It was a black community, and nobody offered to help; I can remember them just staring from the porches. And up the street I saw a car from a TV station stop. A guy opened the door and says, "Jump in quick." It was heaven to see that car there.

marchers in Birmingham did as much as anything to transform the national mood and make legislation not just necessary, which it had long been, but possible." Later that year Charles received an award from the American Society of Magazine Photographers for his civil rights coverage. At the ceremony, Senator Jacob Javits, a liberal Republican from New York, credited his Birmingham photographs with helping to speed passage of the landmark bill.

Moore took this photograph of rock-throwing high school students in Jacksonville, Florida, just moments before they charged him and forced him to flee.

Shortly after Jacksonville—on July 2—President Lyndon Johnson signed the Civil Rights Act of 1964, which outlawed discrimination at the polls and in schools, public facilities, and places of employment. By then Charles's Birmingham photographs had become so much a part of the public memory of those events that they even received some measure of credit for the passage of the legislation. As the historian Arthur Schlesinger, Jr., later said, "The photographs of Bull Connor's police dogs lunging at the

For Charles it was a gratifying moment, for his experience in covering Birmingham had always had special meaning for him:

Birmingham was in my own state. These were my people. I don't give a damn how corny it sounds: my father and my mother are buried in that soil. I grew up on that soil, my brother and I lived and struggled there, I had children there (and I still do). My father might not have understood the necessity of people pushing so hard to make things change. But he would have been torn apart by the sight of blacks being hurt. So I'm there, and I'm watching the dogs being led into the crowds and the high-pressure hoses knocking people down, and it troubled me, because I love the South. And it opened my eyes to the need for change in the state of Alabama. I saw that we had to become a state for all citizens, that blacks deserved the same kind of chance that I was given.

Nineteen sixty-four was also the year of Freedom Summer, the concerted effort by SNCC to register black voters in Mississippi. Nine hundred volunteers, the majority of them whites from northern colleges, were sent to Mississippi after attending training and orientation sessions in Oxford, Ohio. By the time the first volunteers arrived in the state in June, Charles had already traveled along many back roads in the state, covering the initial voter registration effort that took him to shanties, black churches, courthouses, and storefront offices.

Mississippi was true to form in its reaction to the summer influx. On June 21, just as many volunteers were arriving in the state, a black church in Philadelphia was set on fire, and later that day three volunteers on their way to the town—Michael Schwerner, James Chaney, and Andrew Goodman—disappeared without a trace. By the time Charles, assigned by *Life* to the story, and other journalists arrived in Philadelphia, the community had closed ranks against the outside world, and the high visibility of local law enforcement only heightened the atmosphere of fear and intimidation. When Charles approached Sheriff Lawrence Rainey, who was standing by his squad car on the main street of town, for permission to take his photograph, the lawman reacted with predictable hostility:

When I approached him, I also identified myself as a photographer with *Life* magazine. Maybe that was a mistake. He made it very clear: No way! It was like this: "Boy, I don't want no goddamn pictures of me. In fact, I don't want you to take any pictures in Philadelphia. In fact, I'm not going to be responsible for you or anything you goddamn *Life* magazine photographers do. My advice to you is to get out of this town."

I said, "Sheriff, look, I'm from Montgomery, Alabama. I spent five years with the newspaper there. I'm a southerner, but I'm also a journalist. I'm simply here to cover a story."

"I told you, boy, don't take no pictures of me. Move on."

Of course I moved on, and of course I was scared, but I wasn't as scared physically as I was of being arrested. Also, I had to worry about what the sheriff might encourage others to do. In Philadelphia our cars were followed, and we stuck chairs in front of the motel room door at night.

**7**

In January 1965, Martin Luther King went to Selma, Alabama, to direct the voter registration drive there. Selma was a likely target for civil rights activity. Only 3 percent of its fifteen thousand blacks—a slight majority of the population—were registered to vote; its white power structure was entrenched and

ened by President Johnson's guarantee that a voting rights bill soon would be introduced in Congress, King decided to stage a fifty-four-mile march from Selma to Montgomery to petition Governor George Wallace to protect blacks seeking to register to vote. On the morning of March 7, 1965—"Bloody Sun-

**Moore, his cameras at the ready, awaits the marchers at the Edmund Pettus Bridge, Selma, Alabama, 1965.**

opposed to change, and it had an angry, violence-prone lawman, James G. Clark, as sheriff. Charles was the first photographer sent by *Life* to cover the story. By this time he had been in so many trouble spots that he could characterize Selma rather casually as "a bit of a racist town, not as bad as many others."

King's arrival in Selma set off a round of demonstrations, beatings, arrests, and emotional meetings in Negro churches but did little to convince the city to open its voting rolls to blacks. Finally, embold-

day," as it has come to be known—Charles waited outside Selma near the Edmund Pettus Bridge, where state troopers and Sheriff Clark's deputies halted the marchers. Instead of dispersing as ordered, the marchers bowed their heads in prayer. Then the state troopers charged:

**The troopers ran right into and over the demonstrators; my pictures show that some of the marchers fell, and that the highway patrolmen tripped right over them. At some point, the highway patrol set off some**

teargas canisters, and there was teargas floating all over the place. The police were still trying to chase down individual marchers. There were screams, and it was kind of chaotic. I simply photographed as best I could, although I didn't have a gas mask. I was getting as close as I could get, but my eyes would start stinging so badly that I would have to run back out again to get some fresh air. I got the shots, and then it was pretty much over. The marchers had to retreat.

Following Bloody Sunday, James Foreman of SNCC led six hundred marchers in a related march on the county courthouse in Montgomery; Charles photographed deputies on horseback charging the demonstrators, beating them with billy clubs. The next day, Martin Luther King announced that a federal judge had upheld their right to march from Selma to Montgomery, and on Sunday, March 21, King led more than three thousand civil rights supporters over the now-famous Edmund Pettus Bridge on the way to Montgomery. The five-day march, which Charles covered on a motor scooter, attracted clergymen, celebrities, entertainers, and activists; by the time the group arrived in Montgomery, it numbered nearly twenty-five thousand. While he was covering the events in Montgomery, Charles ran to the roof of the Montgomery *Advertiser* building to get a better angle on a gathering of demonstrators. The paper now was under a more conservative management, and when an executive heard that he was there, he personally ordered Charles off the roof. It was a bitter homecoming for the photographer, and a sign that racial attitudes had hardened further in the one-time Cradle of the Confederacy.

## 8

A month after the Selma-to-Montgomery march, Charles was sent by *Newsweek* to cover the U.S. military's attempt to stabilize the Dominican Republic after the outbreak of civil war there. The unpredictable nature of the fighting made the story particularly dangerous for the press, and Charles realized that the violence was beginning to wear on him:

We were in a plush hotel with no food, no water, no electricity, and heating up c rations we got from the troops. As I sat on the balcony in the dark—I could see machine-gun fire in the distance—I tried to put my life into some kind of perspective. I had seen so much violence, and I had been involved in so much ugliness, and I realized that I needed to do something else. I was also being typed as a photographer who specialized in violence. But I was tired of being involved in violent things. I had proved myself as a photographer, and I knew there was a world out there that I wanted to see. So when I got back to Miami, I bought an around-the-world ticket on Pan Am and didn't come back for eight months.

For Charles, "a new world opened up in the Far East." Charles's travels were interrupted by a two-and-a-half-month stint in Vietnam on assignment for *Life*, during which he shot an essay on the B-52 raids that won an award for excellence from an association of aviation and space writers. For the next twenty years, Charles more or less commuted to Southeast Asia, where he worked out of Singapore for Black Star, the photo agency, on everything from industrial and corporate assignments to travel stories and hard news.

Charles's travels have taken him back to the South many times since the 1960s. In the 1970s a business magazine assigned him to do a story on the "progressive South," concentrating on Birmingham.

The magazine wanted me to show how the city was flourishing economically now that race relations were much improved. Birmingham by this time had black policemen and a black police chief. While I was there, a group from the Chamber of Commerce took me out to lunch. When it came out that I was the one who took the photographs of the riots in 1963, they were fascinated: "You did all that? What was it like? Tell us about it."

When I left Birmingham I felt pride. This was a city in my home state—where I had been arrested, where I had seen violence, where I had been injured—and there had been a turnaround here. Although they had a long way to go in rebuilding race relations and a long way to go for the economy, Birmingham was a better city.

It made me feel good that my pictures had something to do with that.

# POWERFUL DAYS

# MONTGOMERY
## 1958–1960

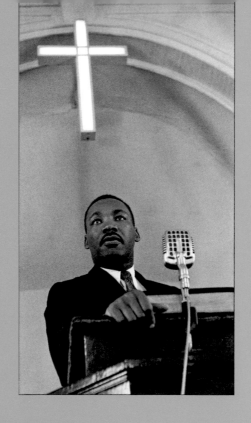

**Montgomery, 1958–1960**

In an ironic twist of history, Montgomery, Alabama, is both the "Cradle of the Confederacy"—where Jefferson Davis took the oath of office as Confederate president in 1861—and the birthplace of the civil rights movement. It was here, in 1955, that a forty-two-year-old seamstress named Rosa Parks was arrested after refusing to give up her seat on a segregated bus to a white man. Local blacks responded by boycotting the city's buses for a year. That historic act of defiance forced the city to integrate the buses and brought Martin Luther King, Jr., pastor of the city's Dexter Avenue Baptist Church, to prominence as a leader of the civil rights movement. Charles Moore began his photography career on the Montgomery newspapers just after the boycott ended; the photographs in this chapter depict the racial tension that continued to beset the rigidly segregated city and the growing civil rights activity there.

A gathering of blacks and whites at Montgomery's Dexter Avenue Baptist Church.

Facing page: Martin Luther King, Jr., addresses a meeting of the Montgomery Improvement Association, which was founded in 1955 to organize the bus boycott. A year later, the city's bus system was integrated.

Facing page, far left: Rosa Parks attends a protest meeting with Ralph Abernathy, King's close friend and associate. By refusing to give up her seat on a bus, Mrs. Parks inspired the Montgomery bus boycott.

Right and facing page: King and his wife Coretta are cheered by followers in celebration of an early movement victory.

Pages 44 and 45: From his pulpit in the Dexter Avenue Baptist Church, King addresses a rapt audience on the need for peaceful protest.

**Left: In 1958, two police officers, unaware of their prisoner's identity, hustle King away from the Montgomery courthouse, where he had been arrested for loitering.**

**Right: As his wife looks on, stunned, King is sprawled across the police desk. After being roughed up and jailed, he was released when his identity became known to authorities.**

A white man swings a
baseball bat at a shop-
per, while another
strikes a black woman
in the background.
The attack in 1960
occurred the day after
black students were
refused service in the
whites-only cafeteria
at the state capitol.

# OXFORD
## MISSISSIPPI
### 1962

**Oxford, Mississippi, 1962**

As the 1960s began, the University of Mississippi was more than the leading school in the state; it was a symbol of the separation of the white and black races. When James H. Meredith, a twenty-eight-year-old black air force veteran, applied to be admitted in 1962, many white Mississippians and their segregationist governor, Ross Barnett, responded with a resounding "Never!" Meredith arrived at the university armed with court papers ordering his admission and accompanied by a small army of federal officers and officials, but students and white vigilantes fought back in a night of rioting that left two men dead and scores wounded. Meredith was enrolled the next morning, October 1, and was graduated in a peaceful ceremony the following August. But, as other pictures in this book show, elsewhere Mississippi continued to shout "Never!" with unabated fervor and tragic consequences.

After the campus was rent by a night of rioting, James Meredith is escorted to registration by Chief U.S. Marshal James McShane and Assistant Attorney General for Civil Rights John Doar. Meredith had spent the night of violence under heavy guard in a university dormitory.

Facing page: Mississippi governor Ross Barnett led the resistance to Meredith's enrollment.

Surrounded by his co-
hort, a law officer
takes a practice swing
with a billy club. The
policemen, identified
by white armbands,
had organized a show
of force to back up
Lieutenant Governor
Paul Johnson when
he turned Meredith
away from the univer-
sity, but they made no
effort to keep the
peace when the riot-
ing started.

Gathering to watch a football game, white Mississippians rally in Jackson, the state capital. They were there to cheer for the Ole Miss football team and support the continued segregation of the university.

Facing page: Jeering Ole Miss students hold the Confederate Stars and Bars aloft.

Pages 58 and 59: U.S. marshals, helmeted and armed, roll into Oxford in army trucks.

**With the pillars of the
Lyceum eerily lit by
headlights from cars
surrounding the build-
ing, U.S. marshals
stand guard on the
steps. Later, as the at-
tacks increased, mar-
shals sallied forth
from the building to
arrest rioters.**

Clockwise from top left: As the riot progresses, prisoners are brought into the Lyceum. One gags into a receptacle from the teargas; the hands of another are cuffed behind his back. Marshals wearing gas masks and helmets stand in a chow line.

A prisoner suspected of shooting at the marshals is frisked.

Facing page: Exhausted marshals line the hallway of the Lyceum. Despite gunfire that wounded twenty-eight of them, they were not permitted to use firearms.

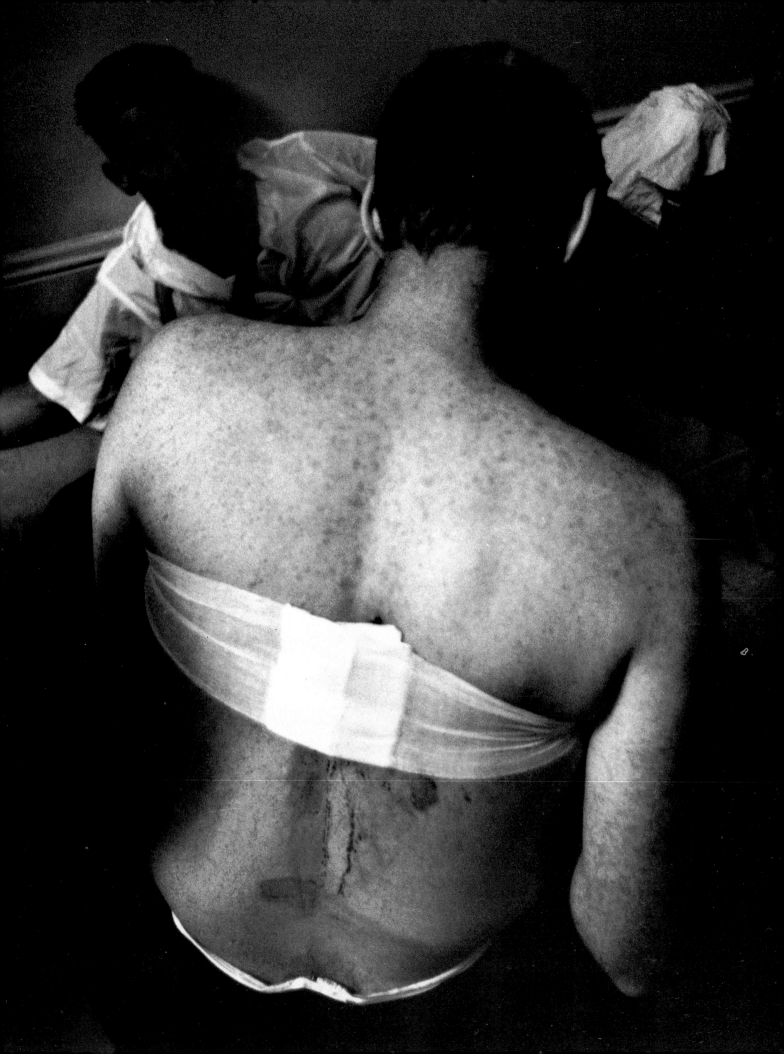

An exhausted and
injured marshal ges-
tures with a hand-
kerchief as he talks to
a reporter. Below, with
his trouser leg ripped
open, another marshal is
treated for a leg injury.

Facing page:
The reporter, William
Crider of the Associ-
ated Press, had been
shot in the back out-
side the Lyceum. He
stayed on the job in-
terviewing marshals.

Early Monday morning, in the aftermath of the riot, a soldier leads a group of prisoners to an interrogation. Less than a quarter of the two hundred people arrested in the riot were Ole Miss students.

Meredith, handkerchief to his nose to protect against the lingering teargas, is escorted to registration—and then to his first class—by Chief Marshal McShane and deputies.

Facing page: The August after he enrolled, Meredith—who had earned college credits in the air force and at Jackson State College—is graduated. The historic ceremony was unmarred by protests or demonstrations.

Still in their city clothes, the marchers gather before setting off. They are, from bottom left, Robert Gore, Sam Shirah, Richard Haley (assistant national director of CORE), Winston Lockett, Eric Weinberger (face partially hidden), William Hansen, an unidentified man (not a marcher), Robert Zellner (foreground), and Zev Aloney.

Facing page: With Sam Shirah in the lead, the marchers leave Chattanooga.

At a press conference before they leave Chattanooga, Richard Haley speaks into a microphone. Fellow marchers Sam Shirah, in hat, and Robert Zellner are to his right. William Moore was unknown before he was killed, but his memorial march attracted the national press.

Pages 76 and 77: Outside Chattanooga, marchers pass along deserted country highways similar to the one on which William Moore was murdered.

The marchers walk through an industrial area on the fringes of Chattanooga.

Facing page: In small towns along the route, young men gather to jeer or simply to gape at the marchers.

Pages 80 and 81: As they reach the Georgia state line, the marchers are met by a phalanx of news photographers eager to record that they had made it this far without being attacked or arrested.

**Left: Outside an antiques store, a marcher shakes hands with two friendly women who offer encouragement.**

**Bottom: As marchers pass a construction site in Georgia, bystanders stare at them with a mixture of hostility and curiosity.**

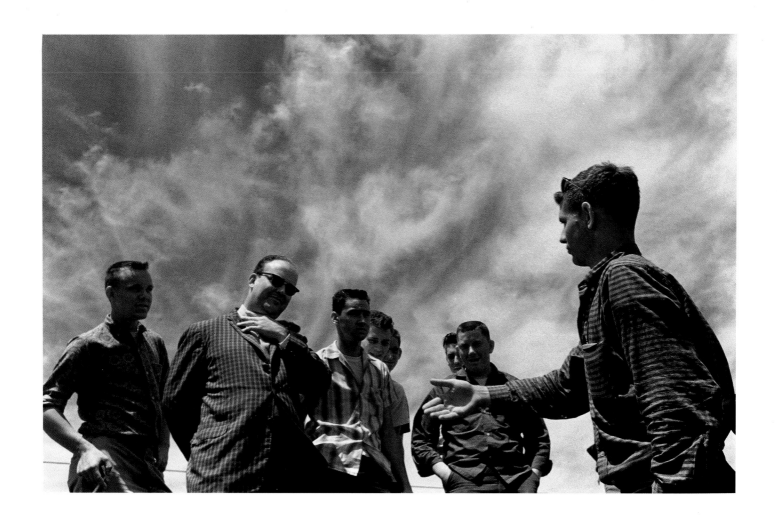

During a rest stop, a group of youths listens while Winston Lockett, seated, facing page, explains the goals of the march. But when marcher Sam Shirah, above, offers to shake hands, a local man recoils in surprise.

A roadside cross bears an ironic message, as each side in the civil rights struggle often claimed that God was on its side.

Facing page: After spending their first night in a small Negro church, the marchers join hands and sing "We Shall Overcome."

# BIRMINGHAM
## 1963

**Birmingham, 1963**

Martin Luther King, Jr., went to Birmingham in January 1963 to lead a campaign against segregation in public facilities, but his efforts there soon became a struggle against Jim Crow in all its insidious guises. In April King was arrested and jailed; on his release he and his aides began training children in techniques of nonviolent protest and sending them forth in orderly groups to be arrested. The strategy filled the city's jails with young blacks and provoked the city's pugnacious police commissioner, Bull Connor, into bringing police dogs and fire hoses into the fray. Charles Moore was there taking pictures for *Life*, and his unforgettable images of jets of water blasting demonstrators and of police dogs tearing into crowds helped put public opinion solidly behind the civil rights movement. Seldom, if ever, has a set of photographs had such an immediate impact on the course of history.

In a confrontation with police and firemen, a group of churchgoers kneels in prayer. Shortly afterward, Bull Connor let them hold a prayer meeting in a nearby park.

Facing page: Bull Connor, Birmingham's feisty police commissioner, outraged the nation by ordering that fire hoses and dogs be used against demonstrators.

Dressed alike in workingmen's clothes, King and Abernathy lead a line of demonstrators to a confrontation with police that they knew would result in their arrest. From solitary confinement King wrote the inspiring "Letter from Birmingham Jail."

Pages 94 and 95: As demonstrators lie on the sidewalk to protect themselves, firemen hose them down with high-pressure jets of water.

A woman, hit from be-
hind and knocked
down by the hoses, is
picked up and res-
cued by a witness.
Another man, lower
right, manages to
keep on his feet—and
hold onto his hat—
during a hosing.

When the water stops,
facing page, he glares
at the firemen, his
face a mixture of an-
ger and bewilderment.

Soaked and still dripping from the fire hoses, a group of blacks, including a young girl, far left, limps away from the scene.

Demonstrators huddled in a doorway seek shelter from the hoses. The water is propelled at a force of one hundred pounds per square inch.

As blacks flee the hoses, a man turns momentarily to confront his attackers.

Cocky as ever—and unaware of how much his actions have aided the civil rights cause—Connor struts through Kelly Ingram Park. Connor urged his men to let whites near the demonstrations. "I want them to see the dogs work," he said.

A man, who uses his shirt to provoke a dog, top, is later chased away (in the bottom picture) by a policeman with his club raised. Most of the protesters in the park stood their ground when the police dogs were called in.

**Above and facing
page: A man looks
calmly over his shoul-
der as a police dog
rips his trouser leg,
then braces himself as
two other dogs attack
him.**

After she is hit at the
knees by a jet of wa-
ter, top left, a young
woman recovers her
balance, then ex-
presses her outrage to
a motorcycle police-
man, below, who is
trying to clear the
park of demonstra-
tors. When he tries to
arrest her, facing
page, she flees,
but she is finally
apprehended.

As a cluster of men in the background struggles against the hoses, a young boy strolls by, erect and poised.

**Black youths, top,**     hoses, then flee,

**take cover behind**     above, as a policeman

**trees in Kelly Ingram**     charges them with his

**Park against the fire**     nightstick.

Adults, top, view the park from the relative safety of a food store. Youths cavort among the rioters, above. For some a holiday spirit prevailed during the demonstrations.

Well-dressed right down to her white gloves, Ethel Witherspoon is wrestled to the ground, top photograph, before being handcuffed and led away. The police officer wearing a necktie is Birmingham Police Chief Jamie Moore.

Facing page: Police drag a woman, top left, to the paddy wagon after they arrest her. Most demonstrators, however, were trained to cooperate with the arresting officers, as the others in these photographs are doing.

In front of a department store, youths taunt a policeman. Once the demonstrations overflowed from the park into downtown Birmingham, the city became willing to start negotiating a settlement.

Pages 116 and 117: Proud, defiant, but still cooperative, two women leading an orderly group of school-age demonstrators give information to a motorcycle policeman blocking their path.

Yet another group of
demonstrators is
hauled off to jail.
Once the door of the
paddy wagon is
closed, a lone hand
grips the bars.

# VOTER
# REGISTRATION
## MISSISSIPPI
### 1963

**Voter Registration, Mississippi, 1963–1964**

In the segregated Deep South, voting was for whites only; Leflore County, Mississippi, was eighty percent black with only one black person on its voting rolls. In places such as this, black citizens were kept away from the polls by fear and intimidation. When civil rights leaders made voter discrimination a target, segregationists fought back with lethal force. The 1963 slaying of the NAACP's Medgar Evers, a courageous advocate of the right of his race to vote, was a prelude of violence to come. The next year's voter registration push, called Mississippi Summer, opened with the murder of three civil rights workers near Philadelphia, Mississippi. The voter registration drive extended throughout the rural South, culminating in the Selma campaign in the winter of 1965. Finally, there was progress: in August, President Johnson signed the 1965 Voting Rights Act, and the next year the Supreme Court ruled all poll taxes unconstitutional.

In the Ebenezer Baptist Church in Sunflower, Mississippi, Scooter Giles, a community leader, urges an audience to attempt to register to vote.

Facing page: Voter registration volunteers picket the courthouse in Hattiesburg. Their signs reflect the spiritual undertones of the civil rights movement.

On June 12, 1963, NAACP activist Medgar Evers was slain outside his home in Jackson. Top: Myrlie Evers, his widow, enters the funeral home. Below: Friends and family.

Facing page: In a show of support that brought together different factions of the movement, civil rights leaders joined the funeral procession.

Martin Luther King, Jr., and, to his left, Roy Wilkins, of the NAACP, are among the leaders heading the procession. The murder of Evers, a leading advocate of voting rights, helped galvanize public opinion behind the civil rights movement. The grassroots effort to register Mississippi's black voters and the murder of three civil rights workers in June of the next year also contributed to the passages of legislation guaranteeing voting rights.

A year after Evers's funeral, civil rights activists made a concerted effort to attack discrimination at the polls in places like the Mississippi Delta. The comedian and activist Dick Gregory leads a line of would-be voters through a black community in Greenwood, Mississippi. Right: A man on a porch swing watches the procession pass by.

Facing page: Barely
visible behind the out-
stretched arms of po-
lice trying to direct
the demonstrators, co-
median Dick Gregory
leads a voter registra-
tion drive. Right:
When he refused to
move, Gregory is
hustled off by police.

Vera Piggy leads
an evening voter
registration class
in Clarksdale,
Mississippi.
Facing page: During
the day in her beauty
parlor, Vera Piggy in-
structs a customer on
voter registration pro-
cedure while she
works on her hair.

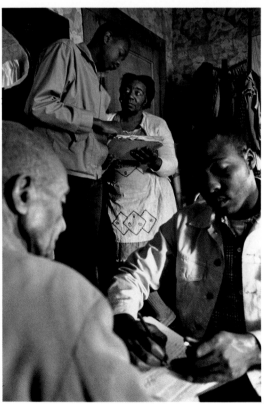

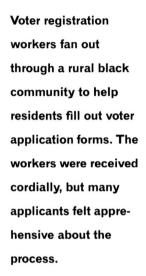

Voter registration workers fan out through a rural black community to help residents fill out voter application forms. The workers were received cordially, but many applicants felt apprehensive about the process.

Facing page: Standing on a porch in the chilly morning air, two voter registration volunteers help a couple with applications. The form then in use asked about criminal convictions and for an interpretation of a section of Mississippi's constitution.

In a community build-
ing that was used as
a voter registration of-
fice, a young activist
prepares to solicit
voters.

Voter registration
worker **George Ball**
explains the voting
procedure to the
mother of three chil-
dren in the family
living room.

On June 21, 1963, three civil rights workers—Michael Schwerner, Andrew Goodman, and James Chaney—were jailed in Philadelphia, Mississippi, where they had been investigating a church burning. On their release later in the day they were murdered. Sailors from a nearby base were called in to help with the search.

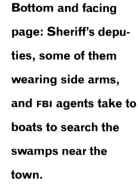

Bottom and facing page: Sheriff's deputies, some of them wearing side arms, and FBI agents take to boats to search the swamps near the town.

**Left: Rita Schwerner anxiously awaits news after her husband's disappearance.**

**Bottom: Otha Neal Burkes, a longtime Philadelphia police-man, is brought in for arraignment in the murders of the slain civil rights workers.**

**Facing page: Philadelphia Sheriff Lawrence Rainey, top, and Deputy Cecil Price, are brought into court in connection with the murders. Price and six other de-fendants were eventu-ally convicted for conspiring to deprive the victims of their civil rights. Rainey was acquitted.**

# THE
# KU KLUX KLAN
## NORTH CAROLINA
### 1964–1965

**The Ku Klux Klan, North Carolina, 1964–1965**

As the civil rights movement gained momentum and strength in the 1960s, so did the Ku Klux Klan, the country's oldest hate organization. The Klan openly burned its crosses and paraded about in hoods and robes; it was also responsible for such acts of violence as the shooting death of Viola Liuzzo, a white civil rights activist from Detroit, after the Selma-to-Montgomery march in 1965. Throughout the 1960s its leaders denied that the organization engaged in violence, and in mid-decade the Klan began to open its rallies to the press in a vain attempt to improve its public image. The Klan was never a primary target of the civil rights groups. As Martin Luther King wrote, "The Negro's great stumbling block is not . . . the Ku Klux Klanner, but the white moderate who is more devoted to 'order' than to justice."

Women of the Klan bow their heads in prayer at a rally near Salisbury, North Carolina. The Klan tried to portray itself as a family organization steeped in godliness.

Facing page: The Grand Dragon of North Carolina, James R. (Bob) Jones, after lighting the fiery cross at a nighttime Ku Klux Klan rally.

**Grand Dragon Jones
drives to a rally with
his Klan robe hanging
in the back seat of
his car.**

**Facing page:
Later that evening
Grand Dragon Jones
attends a Klan rally. A
Confederate flag is
embroidered on his
sleeve. The cross on
the woman's robe rep-
resents the crucifix-
ion; the mark in the
center, a drop of
Christ's blood.**

After the forty-foot cross is lit, the robed men and women circle it with their torches. Then they throw their torches at the base of the cross to end the rally.

In the early evening, Imperial Wizard Robert Shelton, the Klan's highest officer, closes his eyes as he leads the rally in prayer. Shelton was responsible for the Klan's effort to spruce up its image in the mid-1960s.

Facing page: Light from the fiery cross reflects off the robes and hoods of the women.

# THE
# SELMA MARCH
## 1965

**The Selma March, 1965**

In early 1965, Selma, Alabama, became a name as famous as Birmingham in the struggle for civil rights. After a voter registration campaign produced little but violent clashes with authorities, activists set off on Sunday, March 7, for Montgomery to present a petition for black voting rights to Governor George Wallace. Just outside Selma they were routed by police using clubs and teargas. The marchers tried again on Tuesday; this time Martin Luther King, Jr., turned the line around at the police barricade. The following week civil rights activists were savagely attacked by mounted deputies in Montgomery. On March 21—this time backed by a federal court order—King led his marchers out of Selma. Five days and fifty-four miles later, they arrived in Montgomery. "We are on the move now," King told a throng of twenty-five thousand supporters, "like an idea whose time has come."

On a wet, cold morning, marchers trudge along Highway 80 on their way to Montgomery.

Facing page: King and Ralph Abernathy— with United Auto Workers president Walter Reuther, left, and Rev. Fred Shuttlesworth of Birmingham in the second row—attend a memorial service for James Reeb, a white clergyman from Boston, who was killed by white thugs in Selma on the evening of March 9. Earlier in the day, which became known as "Turnaround Tuesday," the marchers made their second attempt to walk to Montgomery but returned to Selma when they were halted by the police.

With Hosea Williams, left, and John Lewis in the lead, marchers move through Selma on their way to the Edmund Pettus Bridge and a bloody clash with state troopers.

Bottom, left to right: Selma's Director of Public Safety, Wilson Baker, a relative moderate, stands in front of Brown Chapel, scene of much of Selma's civil rights activity. Andrew Young leads a group of marchers in prayer. Amelia Boynton, a local activist who was later beaten by police, is at the far right. Facing page: Sheriff's deputies, on foot and mounted, prepare to confront the marchers.

Right: Sheriff James Clark, Selma's notoriously short-tempered and violent lawman, jokes with state police officials before the clash with marchers on "Bloody Sunday." Bottom: State police toting shotguns and rifles prepare to stop the marchers.

Facing page, top: State police wait for the marchers.
Facing page, bottom: Selma police cordon off Brown Chapel to prevent a large group of civil rights activists and supporters from entering.

On Bloody Sunday, Alabama state troopers signal the marchers to halt before attacking them. Marchers first saw the roadblock as they reached the crest of the Edmund Pettus Bridge.

Hosea Williams and
John Lewis lead
marchers toward the
state police road-
block. Lewis was
badly injured in the at-
tack that followed.

Pages 162 and 163:
Almost immediately
after telling marchers
that they had "two
minutes to disperse,"
the troopers charge
with their billy clubs.

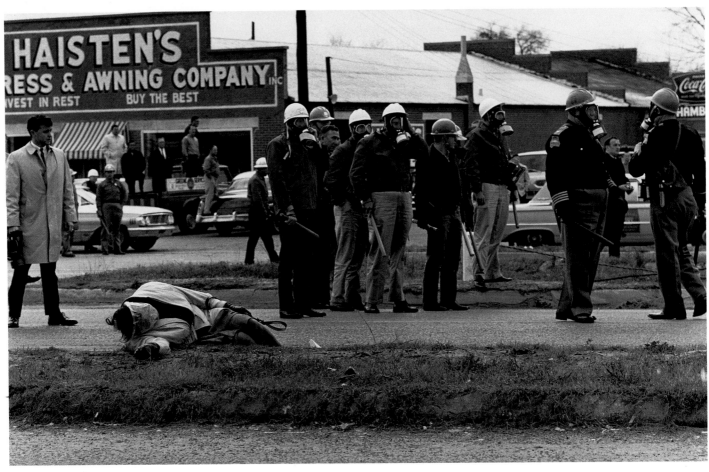

Facing page, top:
In the initial charge,
the marchers topple
like dominoes, some-
times taking the po-
licemen with them.
Facing page, bottom:
State police, joined
now by sheriff's depu-
ties, regroup while

ignoring an activist,
Amelia Boynton, over-
come by teargas and
in the road.

State police wearing
gas masks fire teargas
at the marchers and
then charge them a
second time.

Top: Amelia Boynton, a Selma resident and activist, is helped to her feet after being knocked unconscious by a trooper. "The horses . . . were more humane than the troopers," she said later. "They stepped over fallen victims." Below: A young victim is carried to an aid station.

After the mayhem of
Bloody Sunday,
would-be marchers
are herded back
across the bridge by
mounted sheriff's
deputies.

On March 16, college students gathered in Montgomery in support of the Selma marchers. As they were preparing to demonstrate in front of the state capitol, a mounted posse attacked them. A deputy gestures with his night stick as Pam Clemson, from Juniata College, walks by.

168

**A mounted posseman
brings his club
down on the head of
a demonstrator.**

When a fellow demonstrator is felled by a blow to the head, Pam Clemson rushes to his aid, pulls him to his feet, and angrily points out his wounds to the photographer as the two run to escape further attacks. Clemson, who later described herself as "seventeen years old and out to save the world," was arrested after the incident and held in jail for several days.

A mounted deputy clubs a demonstrator as the attack intensifies. The posse first zeroed in on a small group that was separated from the main body of demonstrators by about a block. It then turned its attention to the larger group and routed it back toward the South Jackson Street Baptist Church.

Harriet Richardson, a student organizer in her senior year at Pennsylvania's Juniata College, presses a cloth to the wounds of Galway Kinnell, who was then poet-in-residence at Juniata. School officials opposed the students' participation in these protests.

Facing page: After the attack, police haul a demonstrator away.

In a melee of horses and bodies, the lawmen scatter the demonstrators. The next day the Montgomery police chief apologized for the attack, and Martin Luther King, Jr., announced that the court had ordered Alabama authorities to allow the Selma-to-Montgomery march.

Governor Wallace did
everything in his
power to stop the
Selma-to-Montgomery
march, only relenting
when the federal gov-
ernment put on the
pressure.

Facing page: Soldiers
and army helicopters
guard the route when
the march to Mont-
gomery gets under
way on Sunday,
March 21.

Behind a truck carrying photographers, the marchers trudge along a wet road. To keep their spirits up, they sang such ditties as: "Old Wallace, never can jail us all. Old Wallace, segregation's bound to fall."

Left: Twenty miles from Selma, the marchers pass a sign that clearly states the distance to their destination.

Facing page: A marcher soothes his tired feet in a rivulet along the road.

Top: Long an active supporter of equal rights for all, folk singer Pete Seeger arrived at the march ready to sing.

Right: Actor Pernell Roberts of the "Bonanza" television series walks with his wife. The couple marched for several days.

Hard-core marchers huddle by an early morning fire. Some three hundred went the entire distance, camping by the road. Other marchers returned to their homes at night or slept in motels.

Volunteers dish out a breakfast that consists mostly of oatmeal and coffee.

Facing page:
The exhaust from a car on a cool morning envelops three marchers in a mist.

"Vote," written across
the forehead of a
young marcher, was a
graphic reminder of
why the march was
being held.

A marcher wears a
sign advertising that
he is from California.
Supporters from all
over the country and
from Canada joined
the march. Right,
Andrew Young, hold-
ing his bedroll,
shivers in the chilly
morning air as the
marchers break camp.

189

As the march nears the end, King— flanked from left by Abernathy, U.N. ambassador Ralph Bunche, and John Lewis of SNCC—leads his followers in a prayer. Below, wearing a flowered lei and new boots, King sits with reporters by the roadside.

James Letherer, of
Michigan, on
crutches, keeps up
easily with his
fellow marchers.

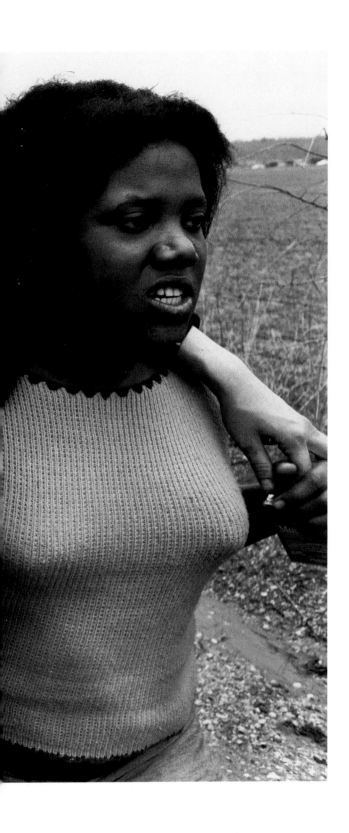

Three young women
sing freedom songs
as they walk toward
Montgomery. The
center marcher wears
buttons of both CORE
and SNCC and another
that reads GROW.

Pages 196 and 197:
As the march picks
up followers toward
the end, King and
Abernathy, together
with black and white
supporters, lead the
procession.

Family members in front of their home watch the procession.

Typically, black onlookers waved enthusiastically as the marchers passed.

Black bystanders
watch the marchers
from the roadside.

Pages 200 and 201:
On the last day, the
march moves along
Dexter Avenue toward
the state capitol.

Many celebrities joined the march to Montgomery and entertained the marchers on Wednesday evening. From left: writer James Baldwin; Mary Travers of the trio Peter, Paul, and Mary; Joan Baez singing with Leon Bibb; and Harry Belafonte, Martin Luther King, Jr., and Tony Bennett.

**Pages 204 and 205:** "We Have Overcome"
In front of the and listen to Martin
Alabama state cap- Luther King, Jr., who
itol, marchers (those told them that "seg-
who went the entire regation is on its
way wear vests) sing deathbed."

# Index

Most of Charles Moore's award-winning civil rights photography originally appeared in the weekly *Life* magazine, for which he freelanced from 1962 to 1972. Since the mid-1960s, he has traveled extensively in Asia on assignment for U.S. and international magazines; he has also won awards for his corporate and industrial photography. In 1989, Mr. Moore, an Alabama native, received the first Kodak Crystal Eagle Award for Impact in Photojournalism in recognition of his coverage of the civil rights struggle.

Michael S. Durham was a *Life* reporter and editor from 1961 to 1972. He is the former editor of *Americana* magazine and the author of two volumes of *The Smithsonian Guide to Historic America*.

Andrew Young worked as a top aide to Dr. Martin Luther King, Jr., during the 1960s. He has served two terms in the U.S. Congress, was U.S. ambassador to the U.N., and was mayor of Atlanta from 1981 to 1989.

Designed by Jim Wageman

The text was set in Cheltenham
and Monotype Grotesque 216 Bold
at Trufont Typographers, Inc.,
Hicksville, New York

The book was printed and bound by
Toppan Printing Company, Ltd.
Tokyo, Japan